Writing Papers
APA-Style

TEN COMMANDMENTS THAT I WISH
SOMEONE HAD TOLD ME BEFORE
I GRADUATED FROM COLLEGE

Bruce A. Shields, Ph.D.

D1472994

THOMSON

™

CUSTOM PUBLISHING

Editor: John Horvath
Publishing Services Supervisor: Christina Smith
Manufacturing Supervisor: Donna M. Brown
Project Coordinator: K.A. Espy
Graphic Designer: Krista Pierson
Rights and Permissions Specialist: Kalina Ingham Hintz
Marketing Manager: Sara L. Hinckley

Thomson Custom Publishing
5191 Natorp Blvd.
Mason, Ohio 45040
USA

For information about our products,
contact us:
1-800-355-9983
http://www.thomsoncustom.com

International Headquarters
Thomson Learning
International Division
290 Harbor Drive, 2nd Floor
Stamford, CT 06902-7477
USA

**UK/Europe/Middle East/South
Africa**
Thomson Learning
Berkshire House
168-173 High Holborn
London WCIV 7AA

Asia
Thomson Learning
60 Albert Street, #15-01
Albert Complex
Singapore 189969

Canada
Nelson Thomson Learning
1120 Birchmount Road
Toronto, Ontario MIK 5G4
Canada
United Kingdom

ISBN 0-759-33858-2

Prologue

I've been on both sides of the podium when it comes to research papers. As a college student, for some 300 years—or so it seemed—I wrote dozens of papers. Some were really good; others I wouldn't have used for a mat in a birdcage. And that was before I was introduced to this intrusive thing known as "APA," and subsequently, APA-style papers. APA stands for American Psychological Association. That really confused me, because I was taking education classes, which I thought had little to do with psychology. Being a confused undergraduate student, I said sort of a bit too loudly underneath my breath to the student falling asleep next to me, "Why do we have to use that style anyway? And for that matter, why do we have to write a research paper at all?" Heck, I wanted to work with people with disabilities, not write a high-brow paper that no one would care about, or worse, no one would bother reading in the first place.

"There are two reasons for this paper, Mr. Shields"—I could hear the sarcasm loud and clear in my professor's voice—"One, when you get to graduate school, particularly for you with education majors, the common denominator for research paper format is the APA-style. Two, I want you to be able to critically think, speak, and write. Got it, Mr. Shields?"

Yeah, baby, I got it!   The temperature in the classroom had climbed to about 240 degrees Fahrenheit. I was sweating through my college t-shirt, but, boy, he had my attention!

This was the start of my journey down the APA-style yellow brick road. Unlike Dorothy, though, I was on my own, and there were lots of lions and tigers and bears, oh my!

And now I find myself on the other side of the podium. I'm actually assigning APA-style papers to my undergraduate (and graduate) students.

When they jump ahead of my reviewing the semester syllabus with them, their first comment is usually, "I've never done an APA-style paper before," or "What's APA?" or "Do we really have to get the manual?" or "Do we get any coffee breaks in this class?"

Then I tell them the minimum number of references they need to cite (there is a difference between that word and "sight" and "site"——and I usually have to go over that) and the minimum number of pages they need to write. Needless to say, we spend a bit of time on the research paper part of the syllabus.

In Piagetian terms, this is called disequilibrium. I introduced into their schemes of development a new dilemma or new information. Their minds were swirling in an effort to assimilate this project and make appropriate accommodations in the way they were thinking. In Shields' terms, I rocked their world.

Inevitably, I take parts of a couple of lectures and briefly go over the APA-style format. I spend a lot of my office-hour time aiding students with topic selection (another disequilibrium occurrence), as well as reviewing paraphrasing, short quotes, long quotes (a.k.a. block quotes), and the listing of references. I joke the whole way through, telling the students that they become experts in the APA writing style after they have turned in their 100th APA-style paper. They are not usually amused.

My motivation for writing this book is that the fall semester has just begun, and as I handed out the syllabus, the "same old-same old" reoccurred. I told the shocked students that I'd go over the APA-style guidelines, actually show them a few pages from papers I have written, and answer any questions, no matter how trivial or, you know, ridiculous.

It was at this point that it occurred to me that, instead of going over this stuff in my lectures (or even to aid my lectures, especially for the visual and reading learners), I should write a sort of "how-to" guide on writing papers. Something like, I wish someone had told me this before I graduated from college——struggling to write in this esoteric style for my professors. If someone had told me, I really believe that my grades would have been higher. I tell my students that they should have in their possession a good, APA-style paper that they can refer to when writing subsequent papers. I grade the papers very hard (and they don't believe this) and very fair. I employ APA-style rigorously, and I want my students to use the same kind of standard when writing their APA-style-papers as I have when reading them. If they make the changes I suggest, their next paper will be easier to write, easier to research, and easier to understand, and it will be easier to apply the APA-style. The same with the next paper and the next and the next. And before they know it, they've written their 100th paper.

Contents

The Ten Commandments, listed in a particular order (ah, that is, mine) are:

I.

Writing the paper will take longer than you think and more research than you will ever imagine.

First things first: Don't give me that bunk about how "I work better under pressure, so I'm not going to start it until the week (or even the day) before the paper is due." Or the rationalization that writing a paper (even a non-APA-style paper) "is a waste of time, fruitless, will not teach me anything, blah, blah, blah."

College students pay good money (well, someone is paying good money) to attend classes, take a couple of notes, participate in a few class activities, take a couple of tests, and get credit for the course. One of the ways to help the professor measure a student's success with all of this is some kind of grade on all of the "gradable" projects. A research paper is one of the best indicators of a critical thinker and one of the best gradable things to do. In many cases, the student chooses his or her own topic (see Commandment II), which is clearly part of the professor's plan for the student to think. This is when the student should show his or her decision-making and problem-solving acumen. For example, if a student really wanted to teach second graders in the inner city, he or she would, in some way, shape, or form, sculpt the research project into something he or she feels very strongly about and in an area that is of sincere interest to them. If the student selects instead, say, the teaching of the American Revolution in England, I would certainly want to know why. Don't get me wrong, I think the American Revolution was revolutionary, and England is my second favorite country, but if the student said it "just" so he or she could "get going on the darned thing," then it will, no doubt be a struggle.

I strongly believe that topics that are "closer to home," and which reflect the students' future ambitions, make the motivation stronger and the research more functional.

Also, researching takes time that the student does not anticipate: computers crash, research materials might not be jumping out at you in the college library, and making copies of the materials is usually a hassle—you gotta have a lot of loose change, the copiers go down, and if the research materials must be secured through an interlibrary loan, that could also take awhile. All research cannot, and in my opinion, should not be done exclusively online. Obviously, using the internet is a great starting place for doing preliminary research, but you have to remember that websites come and go, and securing articles and passages for books takes more time and is more labor-intensive. But journals and texts make the paper stronger and more relevant than do electronic media. The reason is you can secure a permanent copy of something that has been printed. Try finding websites: I've seen them disappear in a matter of days: yes, days! Thus, it takes time to read, research, and secure appropriate references while sifting through all kinds of topical information mostly because books and journals have to be read (there is no "find" or "search" button in the book; we readers know these devices as *an index*).

I'm always bombarded with the inevitable questions: How long does the paper have to be? Does that include the title page, the abstract page, and the references? How many citations do I need?

First question and answer: "How long does the paper have to be?" In my classes, the first paper I assign (ah, to my freshmen) that must adhere to APA is five pages. That is, five pages of text, or body, if you will. Upperclassmen are given an assignment of ten pages of APA-style text. (It's funny, in graduate school papers were a minimum of 20 pages; we graduate students didn't even flinch, when we jumped ahead of our professor reviewing the syllabus with us for the semester. We were like Clint Eastwood: tough on the outside, not a tic about us; but on the inside, we were like Pee Wee Herman: whiney, geeky, and insecure [even without the bow tie]. We just sucked it up, without saying a word, but we were

scared to death.)

Second question and answer: "Does that include the title page?"

Nah, I answer. The title page, which generally has about 20 words on it,

doesn't count!

Third question and answer: "Does that include the abstract page?"

Nah, the abstract page, which generally has between 50–100 words on it,

doesn't count!

Fourth question and answer: "Does that include the references?"

Nah, the references, although extremely important to the strength and

accuracy of the paper, add little to the content of the paper. Nah, oh, I

already said that! Nah, it doesn't count!

Fifth question and answer: "How many citations do I need?" I

don't like doing hard-and-fast rules, because, frankly, it all depends on the

student, how they write, and how in-depth the paper will be. In general,

however, for a 5 pager, there should be a MINIMUM of 15 references.

Something to consider about the rule: I'm not sure I could write that short

of a paper, with only 15 references, but, hey, that's me. And the thing is,

in order to get it to the magic number of 15 references (and this is one of

the mistakes some of my students make—they rely on too few references for their paper), you will probably have to secure at least 30 or so to judge whether or not the references will be citable given the topic chosen.

For example, if the topic is "teaching preparation programs for the instruction of students with learning disabilities," you will come across dozens, if not hundreds, of available references for this very large subject area. The first 15 articles a student finds may not fit the topic. Invariably, however, some students will retrieve their first 15 articles and try to "make them fit." This is not easily done, and when this happens, the references "stick out like a sore thumb." So going back to the rule: Over-search and over-research the topic area. It is better to have too many references and articles that you may not use than to have too few references and cite them over and over and over.

For longer papers, I believe the research should be somewhat sequential. If 15 references are required for a five-page paper, then minimally, the student should seek out 30 sources; if 30 references are required for a 10-page paper, then 60 should be considered, and so on. However, I disagree with the practice of counting references to make sure the student has "the minimum." Further, there should never be a maximum number of references required. Time available, writing style, and final product will determine the maximum number, not the minimum.

Your next move is to kind of set a plan into motion. Sometimes, engaging the professor in this task is something to consider, sometimes not. The "nice" professors are helpful, resourceful, tenacious, and full of ideas and encouragement. The "not nice" professors will tell you—more or less—"there is the library, here is the computer lab, and get your paper in on time. What's your problem?" And that is it. But remember, the professors are unbelievably busy. The handholding thing went out when you graduated from high school.

Anyway you look at it, however, you are on your own eventually. You do have to do the research, you do have to write (and type) the papers, and heaven forbid YOU CANNOT turn in the paper late!! There is actually no problem that you can't overcome, but writing papers still scares you to death. So don't wait for the last minute; get started, today!

II.

Picking the topic isn't as difficult as you think.

When I begin to discuss the topics of the research paper with my students, I often am questioned (and pressured) to just assign the topic, because "I don't know what I want to write about" is the usual refrain I hear. I get peppered with this statement. My wise-guy answer to this is, "Welcome to college. This is where you make choices and live with the consequences." My non-wise-guy answer almost starts out like a Socratic questioning gig:

Student: I don't know what I want to write about.

Professor (me): What are you interested in?

Student: I dunno.

Professor (me): What's your major?

Student: Elementary education.

Professor (me): What grade do you want to teach?

Student: I dunno.

Professor (me): Well, if you could pick any teaching job you wanted, what grade would it be?

Student: Ah, third grade, I guess.

Professor (me): OK, what really interests you about the third grade?

Student: I've always wondered why some classrooms were set up in rows, while other classrooms have the desks facing each other in groups of four students.

Professor (me): Alrighty then, why don't you do some preliminary research on third grade learning environments and see what you come up with?

Now, imagine doing this with each one of the students. It happens in every one of my classes when I assign a research paper. Upperclassmen can be a bit more headstrong in picking their topic because they know what they are interested in, and sometimes, because they have had me in previous classes and they know the Socratic Method routine.

Of course, the student probably shouldn't simply write about the transporting of goods and services to the United States. I don't believe there would be a place for that topic (I don't think) in any of my classes, which typically deal with education, human services, and so forth. Were I a business instructor, I'm not sure I would approve of the student writing about third grade learning environments. See what I mean?

One of the best things that students can do (and I remember when they do this) is come to me with their proposed topic and some of the preliminary research results they have secured. I can then offer my opinion on how to shape the subject area making sure they include key areas we discuss. This approach helps the student to more clearly define their topic and further hone their research efforts. When I have these wonderful (yet, rare) conversations, these students generally will get a higher grade. Why? They are focused, they have their goal in mind, and now it's a matter of doing what I outlined in Commandment I.

APA-STYLE PAPERS

III.

The APA book—although everything is there—isn't as easy to decipher as you think.

When assigning an APA-style research paper to my students, I typically spend part of a lecture or two reviewing the parts of an APA-style paper: title page (and how to do it), abstract (and how to write it), first page of the body (YES, you have to include the title of the paper—the same one used on the title page), the three ways to cite references (See Commandment V), and what the reference pages look like.

I swear, every time I do this little presentation, someone always asks referring to the APA-style manual, "Isn't this in the book?" I always answer that it is and that they should refer to it often. And I define "often" as, it should be written in, pages folded, with a bunch of yellow-sticky memo notes hanging out of it; that is, it should be worn from looking through it often.

As soon as I utter the syllable "yes," my students stop listening and start playing Hangman, until I get back to the "real" content of the lecture.

Sure, everything is in the APA-style manual, but finding it, considering how it will look in the paper, and actually typing it in the correct way aren't as they may appear. There are a few computer-based aids that I'll mention later, but I tell students, don't buy the book and let it sit, especially while writing the paper. I have mine with me constantly while I'm writing. And I KNOW how to write these crazy things. I'm always checking and double-checking to make sure that what I submit to publishers is a consummate and impeccable piece of work as possible, that is, you know, the best of my ability.

Now, don't get me wrong. Adhering to APA-style isn't that easy, especially when you're first learning what an APA-style paper is. But, in time, you'll be able to look at the pages on paper or on the computer screen and just know that something looks out of whack and you'll be reaching for your APA-stylebook. I appreciate the effort that students, particularly emergent research writers, make to use proper APA-style correct.

When I played college lacrosse, our coach would constantly drill into us this notion about effort. He would tell us, "You want to make errors of commission, rather than omission." I thought the expression was kind of neat because it rhymed. So, during one of our practice breaks, I approached the old coach (he was six years older than me) and asked him to explain the commission-omission thingy. He told me that he would never get riled if a player tried to complete a play by being in the right place, with the right screen formation, with the right pass, and with the right shot. He went on to say that performing at a point of authority and mastery, even if the play didn't work, was tied to a player's best effort. Then he got a big ol' scowl in his face. His voice became much more serious when he said, "But, making an error of omission means that the player didn't really give it 100% effort. He basically had no idea what he was doing and he shouldn't even have tried."

Thus, concluded the first real learning experience of my freshman year.

I use this commission-omission method of teaching the APA-style and grading the papers. I look to see how the students performed the task, of not only completing research and shaping the paper in useable productive sentences that make sense, but also to see how APA is applied. And, trust me, it is really easy to pick out the students who are at the "commission" level and who are at the "omission" level.

In regard to the computer-based APA devices that are currently on the market, there are several that are useful, but they should NEVER take place of the book. Get it, know it, be it: APA-style Publications Manual (whatever the latest edition is will do). One device is known as the APA-Style Helper (whatever the latest edition is will do as well). The Helper is actual software that you load in your computer, and as you're writing your stuff, it will format references and provide a template for the manuscript outline. There is also a study guide that aids in the citing of electronic resources.

A word of caution: The manual, the software and the study guide are ok, but don't rely on them for checking to make sure the paper is written in APA-style, that the grammar is correct, that there are no spelling errors and that you have written a good quality paper. Only YOU, the author of this paper, can do those things; you are responsible for its academic accuracy and scholarly appeal. Shirking this responsibly is clearly an error of omission, and your paper should be graded accordingly: with the sobering consequence of not too good of a grade.

I should mention one little sidebar about italicizing v. underlining in the reference section of the research paper. The latest edition of the APA-style manual shows that the references are typed with italics when giving the title of a text, for example. When I wrote my dissertation, the correct procedure was to underline the various titles of books and journals.

Underlining, to me, makes the titles jump out and easy to read. Italicizing, especially if the student is printing out the 31st draft of the APA-style paper at 4:37 AM, is difficult to read. So the word of caution is to make sure that italicizing is used. Without it, an error of omission has occurred. I like underlining better, but computers today make it a breeze to italicize, so I guess that's why the Big Cheeses at APA use it. When I'm elected to the Big Cheese status at APA, I'll change it back to underlining. Ah, don't hold your breath; in the meantime, employ the italicizing button on the tool bar of your word processor.

IV.

Say "good-bye" to informal phrases and "I won't see you around as much" to pronouns.

When I was in graduate school, we were often instructed to give examples and non-examples of things. (We didn't use the words "examples" and "non-examples." No, no, no; they weren't scholarly enough.) We had to use the words "exemplars" and "non-exemplars." No real difference—they mean the same thing! I just think graduate students and definitely the tenured professors like the sound of the latter words. Using this notion of exemplars and nonexamplars, a student is able to clearly discover and discern the subtle and not-so-subtle differences between two things. Suppose, for example, you are about to teach a science class in the topical area of "hardness." You, the instructor, should have a piece of talc and a piece of granite. The talc is soft and can easily be broken and chipped using just your fingernails. The granite, which is very heavy and dense, cannot be chipped with your fingernails. In fact, you'd probably scratch and break your nails if you tried.

See the difference?

In introducing this chapter, I'll give some examples of informal phrases—which should not really be used in an APA-style paper—and some examples of how to say the same thing, only in a more formal way.

EXAMPLE OF INFORMAL PHRASE

"If you were like, teaching a kid that had LD, you would pretty much know what to do with her during one of your lessons even if the kid didn't know what you were teaching."

EXAMPLE OF MORE FORMAL PHRASE

"Instructing any student who has been diagnosed with a learning disability will require much attention from the teacher, especially during an activity that is unfamiliar to the student."

See the difference?

This leads me to my next point: the use of pronouns. Let me state, unequivocally, that I adore pronouns. You know the way they are used to substitute for nouns or noun phrases and the way they designate persons or things previously specified or understood from the context in the writing. But remember that these words (i.e., you, she, him, her) really have a very limited place within the APA-style research paper.

Pronouns make this type of scholarly paper too informal, and they should be avoided as much as possible. They can also make a sentence confusing. For instance, look at the above example of the informal phrase. The "you" is the teacher, but without reading it a few times, I might think that the "you" could also be the student. Yes, you can argue with me, but isn't the more formal phrase—the one without the pronouns—much clearer?

If you do use pronouns, then you must ensure that they adhere to APA-style: they must agree to singular or plural usage, and (may be used as either subjects or objects).

V.

There are three ways to cite in APA-style.

Citing references in the context of an APA-style research paper can be done in only three ways: paraphrasing, short quotes, and long quotes. Because of this, I don't understand why students fret so much when it comes to writing one of these APA-style bad-boy papers. Once you've learned the three ways to cite, the next "trick" is to mix up the three throughout the paper. When done correctly, citing really makes the paper a strong piece of academic and scholarly work that will more than likely receive a high grade. Why? Because the student picks a topic of which he or she finds of interest. The student then shapes whatever argument or statement is being made with the use of previous authors' research results or published works. Does this sound too good to be true? It's not!

Paraphrasing, as defined in the Shields' lexicon, is simply restating what an author has said in YOUR own words. Say, for example, you come across the following in an article: "Most teachers of students with disabilities have earned master's degrees and have tenure." Paraphrasing and citing it in the paper would look something like, "According to Smith (20XX), students with disabilities will have experienced and well-educated teachers." Or, it may look like this: "Students with disabilities will have experienced and well-educated teachers (Smith, 20XX)." Both statements say basically the same thing; the only difference is how Smith's statement is paraphrased. Why paraphrase at all? Because you are shaping your argument or statement using the work of other authors to give credence to the point you are making to the reader. Your argument is malleable, and you are reinforcing your viewpoint through the use of previous work. This makes your paper stronger and a better piece of scholarly work.

Another way to cite authors' work in an APA-style research paper is through the use of short quotes. This type of citation involves using a word-for-word quote from an author. This type of quote must contain FEWER than 40 words. A short quote is woven into a paragraph that includes the author's name, the year that the work was published, and the actual page number(s). A short quote drives home the thoughts and arguments of the student's paper. If done correctly, not only can it congeal the subject matter, the short quote can also be used to move from one theme of the paper to the next.

Here is an example of a short quote and how it would look in your paper: Smith (20XX) states that,"the brief fall did not injure the child, but embarrassed the parents (p. 116)." _**Or:**_ The warning from the skies "was a sure sign that the hemisphere was responding in cataclysmic ways" (Jones, 20XX, p. 123). _**Or:**_ "The barber was really the lookout for the gang" (Howard, 20XX, p. 75).

Remember that these quotes would be included in the paragraphs you have written to expand or reinforce your point. Of course, you can also use these quotes to offer different opinions within your paper; this is another way to let the professor understand that you know what you're writing about and that you have researched your topic area well.

The final method for citing references in APA-style is known as long quotes. A long quote includes 40 words or more. They are indented and have no punctuation at the end of the section. Also, at the conclusion of the long quote, the next paragraph is NOT indented. Here is an example:

The notion of cloud movement is clearly involved with the rotation of the world on its axis. Smith (20XX) defines rotation as:

> The process of movement that, seemingly, is stationary even when this is not detectable by human senses or any mechanical equipment. There also seems to be a cycle of changes that are not detectable, but which certainly coincide with all four of the

seasons of a metrological year for which there are no beginnings

and no endings. (p. 10)

According to a New York City research firm, clouds will be white, gray,

and pink, depending upon the axis and the position of the sun...

Often, my students will ask me how many of each of these three

citations methods they should use. There is no concrete answer to this

question; it depends on the length of the paper, the topic, and the writing

style of the author. Long quotes take up more space in a paper, while

paraphrasing and short quotes take up less. Too many long quotes, and I

would question how much the student had actually written; too few and I'd

wonder how much research had been done.

I tell my students to use a combination of the three methods. I like

to see a few long quotes, more short quotes, and more paraphrasing than

anything else. I'm also very interested in what the student has to say and

how they weave in all three citation methods with how they write too.

That is, the student's writing style and how all three citations are used to

support the author's arguments make for a very strong, or in some cases, a

very weak paper.

VI.

Keeping up with new media is important, but

difficult to cite.

Citing authors of books is cake; articles are a little trickier, along with ERIC articles (ERIC stands for Educational Resources Information Center, but almost no one knows what ERIC means, unless you're a geek...like me).

Even multiple authors of all of those resources aren't as difficult to format, once you get the hang of it. Like the new way, like, (as my daughters say) is how to cite URL's—ah, that's the place where you type in a web site that usually begins with: www.; or http.; or whatever (as my daughters say) and you are instantaneously sent to a website that has all kinds of stuff on it, that may be very useful to include in a research paper. By the way, URL is an acronym for Uniform Resource Locater; not many people know that. You could impress your friends and relatives by laying that one on them at your next family get-together!

One of the problems (and for me my biggest pet peeve) with URL's, just as with a person's putting stroke, is that they come and go.

Unfortunately, when the URL disappears, the reference is usually gone forever. As a researcher (or geek, as my daughters call me, but I've already mentioned that), this is very disturbing. If a book is needed for a research paper and is old, I mean really old, like John Dewey's 1910 classic *How We Think*, a musty, decrepit copy of it can still be found someplace in an educational library. I like that a lot. Because, as you know, books and articles and studies and literature reviews are all available with black ink and white paper that can be read while holding them in your hands. Electronic stuff sometimes vanishes like childhood innocence.

As a researcher (or geek, as my daughters continue to call me), I sometimes like to "check" on student work by actually looking up their references that they have cited. When an electronic citation is listed, I retrieve the URL to verify where the student got the stuff and see what is there. I look to see if my student has paraphrased it correctly, cited it correctly, and used the author's work in the way it was intended. Now, don't get me wrong, I typically assign an APA-style paper to over 100 students in any given semester, and of this number, I usually verify citations on only two or three student papers each semester (This drives the students crazy because they just don't know whose paper will be "checked.") As a side note, my students can't believe how strict I am about applying APA-style (or anal, as some of my students call me). But I passionately believe in the tenets of the APA-style because it makes the paper orderly, well-researched, well-written, and well-edited. Not applying APA rules correctly really jumps out at me while I'm reading the research papers; so, for me, the paper is easy to grade and easy to give constructive feedback. I tell my students that this is my job: grading stuff and putting feedback on stuff. They ask if I can grade it easy (or better yet), they ask if the paper can be less of a percentage of the overall grade. I really like my students, but giving them an "easy" grade or having the paper "not count as much" for the overall grade will only hurt them in the long-run. To do otherwise would short-change their educational knowledge and my educational responsibilities to them.

So, I just say, "no."

Thus, it is a matter of great importance to apply the rules of the APA-style manual correctly. Unfortunately, the new media of electronic materials isn't as cut and dried as simply citing the Dewey-guy's book. The APA-style is very difficult to follow, and in my view, the book is often inconsistent. I used to think that it was "just me" and my analness (if that's a word), but I work with an expert—a reference librarian at the college where I teach—and we're always talking and questioning and debating about the proper citation format for electronic sources. It's just not very clear. I wonder if she thinks I'm a geek or anal, hmmm.

If the website you are using includes the author's name on the web site, then you would cite it just as you would a book or article: name of the author and the date. In the reference page, it's not all that tricky. If the reference is online, you would cite it like this:

Smithworthy, A. B. (1999). *Do teachers really have fun in the classroom?* Retrieved June 16, 2002 from http://www.smithworthy.com/webbriet.html

When citing short or long quotes from websites that don't have page numbers (and most of them don't), you will have to be a bit more descriptive in the text by including the paragraph symbol ¶ or the abbreviation "para. x." To illustrate, say short quote you wanted to use was: "Common knowledge had always been that 'teachers were more fun on Thursdays than was previously thought'" (Smithworthy, 1999, ¶ 7). Or you could use (Smithworthy, 1999, para. 7). If I was going to confirm that short quote, I'd type in http://www.smithwothy.com/webbriet.html, then I would count down seven paragraphs, and I should find the phrase, "teachers were more fun on Thursdays than was previously thought." If it's not there, then there could be a problem.

If the website has a date on it, include it in the references with year, month, and day, as in (1999, March 15). If not, just put the year, like the above example.

If there is no date, use (n.d.) in place of the (1999) above, got it? That includes both in the text, as well as the reference page. Do not, however, put the month and date in the text!

Now citations are a little trickier when there is no author's name listed, but fret not! Here are a few CORRECT citations of the most frequently used electronic media and URL's as they should appear in the text of the paper along with how they should appear in references.

Say your text goes something like this:

"Nation-wide groups and organizations have advocated for programs for people with disabilities to live in as normal a place as possible (The Arc, 1997)."

The reference would look like this:

The Arc (1997, July 17). *Milestones.* Retrieved October 25, 2000, from http://www.thearc.org/misc/milestone.html

With regard to italics, if the citation is from an online journal, then italicize the name of the journal. If it is from a website, italicize the name of the web page or the title of the article from which you obtained the information. Look at the above, "Do teachers have more fun in the classrooms?" and "Milestones." You do notice they are italicized, right?

Another example would look like this: As stated by Willard-Holt (1999), "in order for these children to reach their full potential, it is imperative that their intellectual strengths be recognized and nurtured, at the same time as their disability is accommodated appropriately" (Para. 1). For this one, since there is an author, the reference would appear thusly:

Willard-Holt, C. (1999). *Duel exceptionalities.* Retrieved November 9, 2002 from http://eric.org/digenst/e574.html

Now do you see the one constant? If you remember anything from this book, remember this: the thread from the text to the references and the references to the text in the above examples are Smithworthy, TheArc, and Willard-Holt. If the author's last name or the website is listed in the text as citation sources, that's the direct link to find them in the reference section. Man, you just got the whole gist of this electronic media stuff with a cherry on top!

VII.

Look at professional journals that publish in APA-style.

It is one of the best things to do; it is one of the worst things to do. Sound familiar? With apologies to Charles Dickens, I introduce this chapter with what to do, and what to look out for, when you're reading journals and books. Sometimes, believe it or not, the publications do not adhere to the strict application of APA. That drives me crazy!! Because as I'm up on my mountain pontificating all the good and righteous requirements to follow to make for a good and righteous APA-style research paper, seeing even one article, or one book with improper citations or reference format, ruins the whole day!

Imagine some smartsy-smartsy college kid bringing me an article that doesn't adhere, with the axiom, "If these professional journals don't stick to APA, why are you making us?" I'd clear my throat a couple of times, hoping that the sun would burnout before I answered. Knowing that my chances of the sun imploding, however thin, would save me from answering Mr. or Ms. Smartsy-Smartsy; of course all mankind would be wiped out, just to save me from explaining, and then I'd mention something about me being the "captain of the ship," and thus, in complete control of what happens on deck. Within this confusion of the sun and of the captain's schtick, I do explain that, even if they say they conform to APA standards, sadly, some publications simply do not. That tempers, to some degree, my reliance on looking to journals and books to provide examples of proper APA usage. I also tell my students that with their critical eye and after they have written their 100th paper, they will notice quite easily when APA isn't applied as it should. I tell the students that I used to read textbooks for the joy of learning and expanding my horizons (it is at about this point they begin to hold their sides from giggling so hard that they fall out of their seats), and now I read textbooks to see if there is tight adherence to APA. Happily, I tell them, most do a pretty decent job; others take more of a liberal approach.

Nonetheless, looking at professional journals and textbooks gives the student a very good example of how they are written and what they look like in black and white print.

I've been reading the "newer" editions of existing journals to see how they handle the citing of electronic media. Although they do not say it, I believe some will not accept papers or articles that include electronic citations. Not only is this a missed opportunity for my students, I also believe that some editors are not allowing for the realities of current research. In my opinion, you cannot deny the present by holding on to the past; this sounds like another quote from Dickens! (Check out *A Christmas Carol*. Look up what happen to Fezziwig's business philosophy and see what ole' Scrooge did to him.)

A "seasoned pro" such as myself can just scan an article's citations or look at the reference section of a journal or a book and be able to tell if the text is written in APA-style or not. But the definitive sign is peeking at the contributor/author guidelines, which instruct potential writers on how to submit their work.

This leads me to a rather apparent observation: If the guidelines instruct the author wannabe to submit APA-style, then don't submit your work in ASA or Chicago style. I would imagine that would make editors crazy. They do not have the time to convert work from one style to another. This is especially true when it comes to refereed journals—that is, articles are sent to journals, the editors send them to specialists in the field, and these readers, actually "vote" on whether it is worthy to be published. Editors get so many submissions that, even if the article is well-researched and well-written, the author might get a quick and curt rejection letter. Particularly for someone who has to publish to survive, adhering to the correct writers' style is a "must."

Against my better judgment, I am offering a list of journals that purport to publish in accordance with APA-style. The list is not exhaustive; it simply contains just a few of the journals I have come across that "do" APA-style. I say "against my better judgment" because I am in no way endorsing these journals. However, I know that someone, somewhere, will say, "Oh, yeah, that Shields guy writes about APA-style journals and doesn't even include 'X' journal; I don't think he has a clue." Well, I do have a clue, but I'm not going to list EVERY journal that conforms to APA-style. I do have to prep for classes and be in my office during office hours, you know.

Here is my list:

American Journal on Mental Retardation

Mental Retardation

Psychological Bulletin

Psychological Review

Teacher Education and Special Education

Young Exceptional Children

VIII.

APA is different than any other writing style but a few sub-Commandments apply.

In addition to the APA-style that is used by students in the social and behavioral sciences, there are many other writing styles, and thus many ways to cite references. That's not to say that some suggest (and debate) that various professors in social and behavioral sciences don't use different writing styles; they certainly may. What the student must realize, however, is that if the professor demands a specific writing style for papers (and believe me, they will: look at the syllabus), then the student must conform. No big deal, really. But if the student doesn't know the style well, or has never heard of it, the onus is on the student to become familiar with it. Period. Welcome to higher-education!

Let me now editorialize a little; actually, I've been editorializing the whole way, if you haven't noticed, so why stop now?

When I assign an APA-style research paper to my students, particularly to my freshmen, they usually look like they've just watched a "Twilight Zone" episode. (A few of my upper classmen sometimes do this as well.) It's not a "deer in the headlights" look—they're not scared, but it was like I had just started talking in Latin, backwards. The first couple of times this happened, I thought I had shocked them, and I suppose I did.

Then the rush of comments about "why," "what for," "don't know how to do this," "this is dumb," "we never had to do this in high school," "no other professor in the education department has ever assigned me a paper," and so on and so on and so on. When I was a rookie assistant professor, I would diligently try to answer each question in the hope that understanding equals motivation. But it seemed like the more I explained, the less I was helping students to gain a level of deeper understanding. Thus, I was reminded of the words of some philosopher, whose name escapes me: If you're explaining, you're losing!

So instead of whining to the professor, the best thing that the student can do is ask what references and resources he or she would recommend in order to become familiar with the required writing style. Better yet, ask the instructor what references he or she uses while they're writing. I love being asked that; maybe they're just sucking up, but assuming that the professor has written their 100th paper in the style they have just assigned, they should be able to rattle off a list of sources right off the top of their head. This should give the student some level of comfort. If the professor can do it, certainly the student can learn it and do it as well. Remember, you're not the first student in history to have to write a research paper.

The different styles are known as:

ASA (American Sociological Association)

Turabian/Chicago Manual of Style

MLA (Modern Language Association)

CBE (Council of Biology Editors)

Government Publications

Legal Citations

Medical Citations

Regardless of the particular style used, you must do the following:

*Hit spell check, but don't rely on it. The spell check has many, many plusses, especially for people like me who can't spell to save their lives. Spelling was a very difficult area of my academic career. If I had had spell check as an undergraduate, I firmly believe that my grades would have been higher. But after typing the paper, on real typewriters with real paper over and over and over again, I just didn't care about fixing the "typos" as I was doing my proofing (pretty much when I was walking it to the professor to hand it in). I was envious of my fellow students who could not only write and research well, but who could spell as well! The negative side of spell-checking is that it makes the author less concerned with looking for misspelled words. Besides, why would I have to be concerned once the little box comes up that says, "The spelling and grammar check is complete"? You click on the "OK," print it, and hand the sucker in, right? Well, there is a difference between martial and marital; there is a difference between their, there, and they're; there is a difference between to, two, and too. All wonderful words, but hardly interchangeable!

*Make sure grammar check is employed as well, but don't rely on it. Grammar check offers suggestions on how best to say something, making sure that the structural relationship between the uses of language is intact. Your sentence, as you have written it, might work very well, but at least the grammar check asks you to make a decision about what you have written and possibly to improve it. Then, to be on the safe side, take a look at it. You know why? If we're writing correctly, considering all kinds of things that a writer/researcher must consider, it makes you stop for a second and it makes you consider to render a decision about what you've written. It's a shame that grammar check can't do that with all sentences; it would greatly assist both the student and the professor!

*Make sure someone reads your paper; ah, your last draft, not the first, but don't rely on this. You'd be amazed when I get done grading a paper. I'll have a conversation with a student and I'll sometimes ask how many drafts he or she had written. The answers vary from one to about fifteen.

The "one draft and hand it in" cracks me up and they are easy to grade. Fifteen drafts is a little more troubling. When someone writes something over and over and over, he or she get too close to the written work and doesn't "see" very simple errors that pop out, often missing them. Having someone read the paper, especially when it's pretty much the last, polished draft, will reveal things that the author cannot "see:" Omitted words, omitted punctuation, or misused and different words with similar spellings, like "martial" v. "marital." Just have your buddy circle the errors and then you can plough through them when you're making corrections.

*Find a buddy who is an English major to read through your paper, but don't rely on this reader either. Although the English major could really strengthen your final product before you hand it in, you really should take a hard look at his or her feedback. That's not to say they are wrong, but when it comes to applying all of the rules of the English language, you may have been doing something for years, and it takes an expert to point out something that you didn't realize you were doing. For me, I didn't get this pointed out to me until graduate school: the use of the words "less" and "few." Not that I want to get into an English thing here, but the correct phrase is fewer lashes (things that can be counted) causes less pain (things that can be measured)!! It's sort of a complicated rule, but once the English teacher/reviewer pointed this out to me in one of my papers, I had an existential moment, one that will stick with me for the rest of my writing career, which, I hope, has a few more years to go; gotta love the English language.

*The reason I have stated over and over not to rely on anyone or anything is that, as I stated in Commandment III, you are the author; you are responsible for your paper's content, accuracy, and academic integrity. You cannot "blame" anyone for not picking up anything missed or for the grade you received. You see that person in the mirror. For good or bad, that image, has the final say as to what is handed in. Abdicating that responsibility tells the professor that you're only joshing yourself about being a true professional. Stated differently, only you get credit or criticism for your work. Period.

IX.

Paper content and APA-style format seem to be opposed to one another.

When I first began to return graded papers to my students, I heard some grumbling as they were on their way to the next class. It went something like, "He didn't even comment about the paper, its content, my research or anything else; he only graded the APA part!"

Hmmm, I thought, did I really do that? I had to admit that grading these papers was difficult, since I couldn't concentrate on the paper so much because by the time I corrected the English and circled the typos and misused words, and noted the real lack of following the APA-style, I probably didn't concentrate on the content as much as I should have. But I thought about it for a long time, and I have since modified how I grade research papers. I now include grades for both the scholarly content and the application and adherence to the APA-style.

In concentrating on student feedback, my conclusion went something like this: A strong, well-written paper gives the best opportunity for the student to show their APA acumen. I concluded that a paper adhering to APA guidelines increases the chances of a strong paper.

It would follow, then, that a poor research paper, more than likely, does not adhere to APA-style. Before you raise your hand in protest, I will admit that I have read very good papers that were not prepared in APA-style. That's sort of called "plagiarism." I am not saying that the student meant to copy, or worse steal, someone else's idea, but he or she may not have been familiar with the proper use of APA. So if a student doesn't know how to apply APA, then, by definition, the paper would be classified, by me at least, as a weak paper.

Conversely, I've seen papers that adhere to APA-style that were written so badly that they just soured the academic experience for everyone.

Neither of these types of papers will receive a good grade. The highest grades, as my students will attest, are awarded to the papers that are well-written, well-researched, and the "old college try" is attempted at applying APA. The students who write these papers will win every time.

X.

You need to write in APA-style in graduate school.

All right, I've assigned the paper, and the students are shocked; they can't believe they have a paper to write, much less in APA-style. Sooner or later, I get the big fat question, "Why do we have to write in APA-style," and my favorite, "Why do we have to write a paper at all?"

After counting to 10 (twice), I answer. Through gritted teeth, I enunciate as well as possible: "Because you will have to write APA-style papers in graduate school," to the first question and "because teachers should know how to teach, speak, encourage, motivate, think critically and write," to the second question.

I usually get into a hefty debate after that, but as patiently and as professionally as possible, I dismiss all of the students' objections. It's not that they are lazy at all. I believe the students I have taught are the most motivated and hard-working students I have ever met. (Trust me; they are more motivated and harder-working than I was as an undergraduate—at least in my freshmen and sophomore years.)

I believe the students have a hard time with my answers because graduate school is years (and thousands of dollars) away and because they feel that they already know how to write: well and concisely and with style and heartfelt prose, "so much so that it will make you cry, Dr. Shields," they will say.

That cracks me up! As I've said, however, writing formal, technical papers is much different than winging some essay about "It was a dark and stormy night."

Like it or not, professors pass judgment on how well students write. Students who do not write well will inevitably struggle with their studies. If you're struggling with your studies, it's hard to be motivated about writing. But writing, like riding a bike, can be taught, practiced, and mastered. The problem is, though, that it takes time to be taught, time to practice, and the only way to master writing is to, well, write. A lot. Often.

Conversely, students who are strong writers don't really worry about writing papers, even if they know nothing about APA. Learning APA is also a skill that can be taught, practiced, and mastered. The way to do this is to write a lot of APA-style papers.

Did I mention that you'll be writing APA-style papers in graduate school? You can learn how to write APA-style in graduate school, but plan on spending your weekends in the library and your evenings (into the wee hours, that is) learning how to do it. So why not learn as an undergraduate? I tell this to my undergraduates. They are usually not amused. They're not amused because the future is, well, the future...

Now, what's really cool (in the future) is that students entering graduate school feel pretty good about themselves, and they should. They have their degrees, they're motivated to get a master's degree, they've been accepted, and now they're sitting in class. And guess what? All of the other graduate students (who you are sitting next to, in the future) are feeling good about themselves as well. The thing with all of this good cheer, however, is that these students more than likely have written, practiced, and mastered APA writing. You might have written only one paper and, already, you may be behind the curve. These other students don't bat an eye when the graduate professor assigns a 20-page APA-style research paper. The graduate professors usually don't give you a topic, nor do they approve it. But you have to read their minds and try to find out what kind of paper would interest "them," as well as you, and to earn you a good grade to boot.

There are some assumptions about students in graduate school: They know how to write, they know how to research, they know how to cite, they know how to present, and they know how to solve problems. If you ask your professor at this level for any kind of perfunctory assistance, you might get the old, "there are the computer labs, and there is the library. What else do you need to know?" If this happens, nod your head up and down a lot and then go to the librarian and explain what's going on. Technically, librarians are paid to assist you with your research, and technically, the professor, especially at the graduate level, is not.

So you're asking yourself, just what does this graduate school professor do? Well, he or she is paid to give you feedback (and, you know, the same goes for your undergraduate professors!). Not only should you expect this feedback, you should relish it. Professors are funny; they sort of control your life in your years in school. From the opinions they give, you can choose to accept this feedback, rationalize the reasons you disagree with it, or dismiss it! There are all kinds of consequences, both good and bad, that come with their opinions of your scholarly work; however, you have to be unflappable with their feedback!

I am firmly convinced that everyone has the potential to be a "research geek." Given the proper time, subject, motivation, and tools, you, too, can write, and research, and think with the best of other students sitting around you. I have to tell you that there is nothing more rewarding than getting an "A" on a research paper—with few constructive criticisms on either content or APA-style.

I hope that this book goes a long way in assisting you with the selection of your topic, the research, the writing, and the editing of your APA-style research paper.

Good luck and hit the library!